Handy ~~Guide~~
Durban

PETER JOYCE

Struik Publishers (Pty) Ltd
(a member of The Struik Publishing
Group (Pty) Ltd)
80 McKenzie Street, Cape Town 8001

Reg. No.: 54/00965/07

First published in 1996

ISBN 1 86825 894 7

Every effort has been made to ensure fac-
tual accuracy in this book. However, with
the rapid changes taking place in South
Africa, it is inevitable that the information
will become outdated. The author and
publishers invite any comments for future
updates. Write to: The Editor, Handy
Guide Durban, Struik Publishers (Pty) Ltd,
P O Box 1144, Cape Town 8000.

Managing editor: Annlerie van Rooyen
Editors: Inge du Plessis, Laura Twiggs
Design manager: Petal Palmer
Design and DTP: Darren MacGurk
Cover design: Darren MacGurk
DTP maps: John Loubser

Reproduction by Unifoto (Pty) Ltd,
Cape Town
Printed and bound by Tien Wah Press
(Pte.) Ltd, Singapore

The author and publishers would like to
thank the following persons for their
invaluable assistance:
Durban Unlimited for supplying advice
and information
Natal Parks Board for their interest
and time

PHOTOGRAPHIC CREDITS

Copyright rests with the photographers and/or their agents as listed below. ABPL =
Anthony Bannister Photo Library; PA = Photo Access; SIL = Struik Image Library; NPB =
Natal Parks Board
Adey, S. pp. 19 [SIL]; 43; 53 [NPB] **Balfour, D&S.** p. 34 [SIL] **Bannister, A.** p. 48 [SIL]
Cubitt, G. p. 10 **De la Harpe, P.** p. 55 **De la Harpe, R.** pp. 6; 14 bottom; 18; 22; 23 top;
28 [SIL]; 29; 30; 33; 37; 40 top; 41; 44 top; 45; 52 both; 54; 56; 57; 58 [SIL]; 59 both
[SIL] **Dennis, N.** pp. 36; 40 bottom [SIL] **du Plessis, J.** p. 32 bottom **Hodgeson, F.M.** p.
20 [PA] **Knirr, W.** pp. 11; 14 top; 21; 26-27 [SIL]; 35; 39; 44; 49 [SIL]; 50 [SIL]; 51 [SIL]
Migdoll, I. Front cover; pp. 12; 17; 24 **Von Hörsten, L.** Back cover [SIL]; p. 13 [SIL]
Young, K. pp. 5 [SIL]; 7 [SIL]; 15; 23 bottom; 25; 32 top [SIL]

FOREWORD FROM AGFA

AGFA are delighted to join forces with
Struik Publishers in bringing the **Handy
Guide Durban** to the shelves.
    Along with camera and film, this guide
will prove to be an invaluable companion
to all travellers. Illustrated throughout
with beautiful, full-colour photographs,
this compact book is an ideal way to get
acquainted with your chosen destination.

The handy photo and travel tips, along
with clear, easy-to-follow maps, will help
you make the most of your visit.
    And when your holiday is over, bring
your memories home on AGFA film. You
can depend on our widely available range
of HDC print film or RSX and CTX slide
film to capture the beauty of your holiday
in High Definition Colour.

KEY TO SYMBOLS

🕴 *WALKS, HIKES AND TRAILS*

🐦 *BIRDLIFE*

🏛 *MUSEUMS/MONUMENTS/*
GALLERIES

📷 *PHOTO TIPS*

🏕 *WILDLIFE, NATIONAL PARKS,*
GAME PARKS/RESERVES

🚶 *ENTERTAINMENT/*
EXCURSIONS/LEISURE

🏛 *OF HISTORIC/CULTURAL*
INTEREST

❀ *FLORA/BOTANICAL PARKS*
AND RESERVES

🐴 *HORSE-RIDING/PONY*
TREKKING/EQUESTRIAN SPORTS

ℹ *TOURIST INFORMATION*

🎭 *PERFORMING ARTS*

🎁 *SHOPPING*

🚂 *TRAIN TRIPS/RAILWAY*
MUSEUMS

🏃 *SPORTS*

⚔ *BATTLEFIELDS/MEMORIALS*

🛏 *ACCOMMODATION*

CONTENTS

INTRODUCTION

ANCIENT AND MODERN

Among the Zulu people, Christianity coexists with a body of ancient African belief. This embraces the ancestral spirits, who have a powerful influence on their descendants. Above them, and watching over the people, is Nkulunkulu, the 'great-great-one'. There is also an animistic element in Zulu conviction: rocks, rivers, etc. are endowed with a spiritual presence or 'soul`.

Durban, South Africa's third-largest city and premier sea port, was founded as a trading post in 1824 by a small group of colonial settlers, though it was only in 1835 – when it was known as Port Natal and its population numbered just 30 white males – that a formal township was declared. The settlement was then renamed in honour of Sir Benjamin D'Urban, governor of what was known as the Cape Colony at the time.

Today the metropolitan area, home to more than a million people, is almost 400 km² (249 miles²) in extent, sprawling along the coast to the south, across the Umgeni River in the north and inland, over a ridge known as the Berea and beyond, westward to a plateau that rises some 500 m (1 660 ft) above sea level. Here, on the higher, cooler ground, are some of Durban's more fashionable satellites, notable among which are the suburbs of Hillcrest, Westville and Kloof.

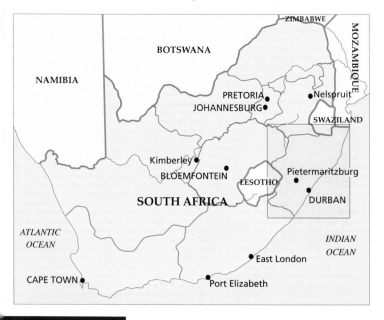

The city draws much of its prosperity from the harbour and the industries it serves, but it is best known to the country at large as a holiday playground, a subtropical paradise for sunbathers and surfers, yachtsmen and anglers and for those who just want to play, laze, eat, drink and be merry in the most relaxing of surrounds.

Durban's beaches, and those of the shorelines fringing the warm blue waters of the Indian Ocean to either side, are among the southern hemisphere's most inviting – long, golden, perennially-sunlit stretches of sand that attract more than a million leisure-bent visitors each year. They are well received; Durban is a generous and stylish host: among and around the gleaming high-rises of the seafront – known as the Golden Mile – are fine hotels, a kaleidoscopic array of restaurants, lively nightspots, entertainment centres, shopping malls, piers and pavilions, elegant promenades, lawns and fountains. Elsewhere you'll find theatres, galleries, museums, quiet parks and gardens bright with flowering plants and, just to the south of the central area, a marvellously exotic world fashioned by the city's Indian community.

Moreover, the region as a whole – the province of KwaZulu-Natal – is both beautiful and fascinating in its scenic and human diversity. This is the home of the Zulu, largest and arguably most distinctive of South Africa's `ethnic groups', a people with a proud and dramatic past and a culture that invites exploration. Along the province's western border are the mighty mountains of the Drakensberg, rising 3 000 metres (9 843 ft) and more above sea level, grand in their immensity, snow-mantled in winter, breathtaking in all their seasons. Descend from the uplands, travel eastwards across the coastal plain, and you will soon reach a land of lakes and game-rich reserves that, together, rank among the premier wildlife wonderlands of the world.

PEOPLE OF THE REGION

KwaZulu-Natal has a total population of 9 million, of whom the vast majority belong to the various Zulu (eastern Nguni) groups. The province is also home to a 800 000-strong Indian community, and to a somewhat lesser number of citizens of European descent. The population of the Durban municipal area was pegged at 71 000 by the 1991 census, but the figure is misleading: metropolitan boundaries have since been enlarged and massive 'urban drift' is dramatically increasing the numbers. Durban is reckoned to be among the world's fastest growing centres, its population expanding at a greater rate than those of Calcutta and Mexico City.

The Golden Mile's fun paddling pools.

AGFA

PHOTO TIP

*If you wish to capture Oriental Durban, try the open-air stalls of **Madressa Arcade**, where you can buy anything from spices to saris.*

ORIENTAL WALKABOUT

This guided weekday walk takes in the commercial hub of the Indian community, including markets selling Indian delicacies, a sari emporium and mosques. Book through Durban Unlimited (see p 62).

Vibrant, cosmopolitan Durban has many faces: the city centre, with its superb cultural, business, shopping and entertainment venues; the Golden Mile, 'where the fun never sets'; the Victoria Embankment, with its waterfront views and historical buildings; the world's ninth-biggest harbour, bounded by the Point in the north and the Bluff with its fine beaches in the east.

CITY CENTRE

Durban's city centre is best explored on foot as most of its attractions are within easy walking distance of each other. Guided morning walking tours, bookable through Durban Unlimited (see p 62) are an enjoyable and fairly quick way of familiarising yourself with the city. On offer are the Oriental Walkabout (left), Durban Experience (see p 11), and Historical Walkabout (see p 12).

A Taste of India

Make your way west from the city centre, along either Victoria or Queen streets, towards Grey Street, and you will find yourself in a different and marvellously exotic world, a place that belongs not to Africa but to the Orient. This is Durban's Indian trading area, the commercial hub of a wider, million-strong community that traces its origins to the ship-loads of indentured labourers brought in, from the 1860s, to work the huge sugar plantations of coastal regions. A number of the original immigrants stayed on after their contracts had expired, and others arrived afterwards to make their homes in and

Slip into a sari emporium on the Oriental Walkabout.

The palatial Jumma Musjid Mosque welcomes visitors.

around the city. Although there are some of its traditions that are slowly being eroded, Durban's Indian society – Muslim and Hindu – remains remarkably integrated and faithful to its cultural heritage.

 Jumma Musjid Mosque

On the corner of Grey and Queen streets you'll see the great golden-domed Jumma Musjid Mosque, the southern hemisphere's largest Muslim place of worship and a friendly-enough place that welcomes visitors of all faiths to its prayer-halls.

Guided tours can be arranged through the Islamic information centre, which is located opposite the Mosque, in Queen Street; tel. 306-0026. The staff at the centre will gladly advise you on places of interest pertaining to the faith. Remember, shoes must be removed before entering the Mosque, and women are asked to dress with appropriate modesty.

 ORIENTAL SHOPPING

For a traditional Oriental shopping experience, try the Madressa and Ajmeri arcades (between Grey Street and Cathedral Road) whose myriad small shops are crammed to overflowing with silver, bronze, brass and ceramic ware, silks and satins, jewellery, crafts, curios and a great deal more. Here the air is evocative, aromatic with the scent of spices and incense, and noisy with the languages and semi-tonal music of the Orient.

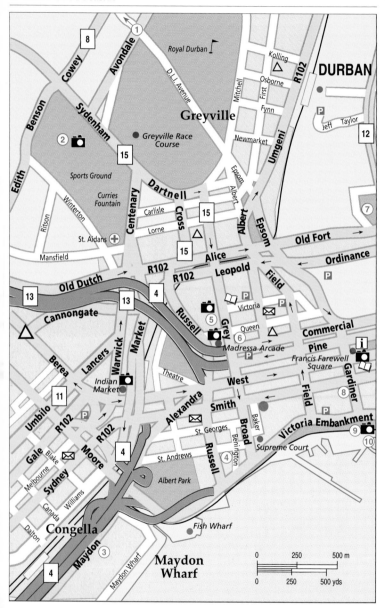

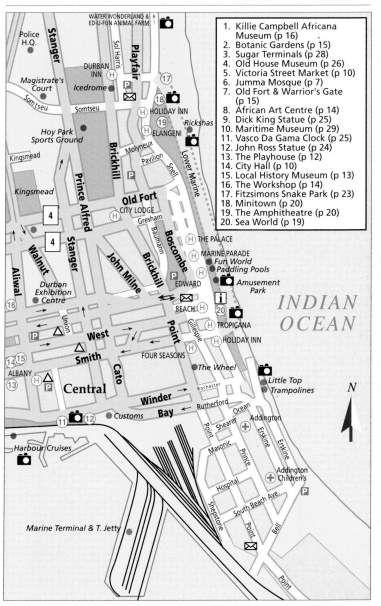

WATER WONDERLAND &
ED-U-FUN ANIMAL FARM

Police
H.Q.

Stanger

Sol Harris

Playfair

DURBAN
INN

Magistrate's
Court

Somtseu

Icedrome

Somtseu

Somtseu

HOLIDAY INN

ELANGENI

Rickshas

Brickhill

Molyneux

Pavilion

Snell

Lower Marine

Hoy Park
Sports Ground

Kingsmead

Prince Alfred

Old Fort

CITY LODGE

Kingsmead

Gresham

Baumann

Boscombe

THE PALACE

MARINE PARADE

4

Walnut

Stanger

John Milne

Brickhill

Durban
Exhibition
Centre

Fun World
Paddling Pools

EDWARD

Amusement
Park

Aliwal

Union

BEACH

Point

Gillespie

TROPICANA

HOLIDAY INN

INDIAN
OCEAN

West

Smith

Cato

FOUR SEASONS

The Wheel

Little Top
Trampolines

ALBANY

Central

Rochester

N

Winder

Bay

Rutherford

Ocean

Shearer

Addington

Customs

Point

Masonic

Prince

Erskine

Erskine

Harbour Cruises

Hospital

Addington
Children's

Marine Terminal & T. Jetty

Shepstone

South Beach Ave.

Bell

Point

Point

1. Killie Campbell Africana
   Museum (p 16)
2. Botanic Gardens (p 15)
3. Sugar Terminals (p 28)
4. Old House Museum (p 26)
5. Victoria Street Market (p 10)
6. Jumma Mosque (p 7)
7. Old Fort & Warrior's Gate
   (p 15)
8. African Art Centre (p 14)
9. Dick King Statue (p 25)
10. Maritime Museum (p 29)
11. Vasco Da Gama Clock (p 25)
12. John Ross Statue (p 24)
13. The Playhouse (p 12)
14. City Hall (p 10)
15. Local History Museum (p 13)
16. The Workshop (p 14)
17. Fitzsimons Snake Park (p 23)
18. Minitown (p 20)
19. The Amphitheatre (p 20)
20. Sea World (p 19)

Explore a curry shop at Victoria Street.

 Victoria Street Market

Worthy successor to the old Indian Market that captivated shoppers and browsers for six decades after it first opened for business during 1910 (it burned down in 1973), this ornate building is surmounted by eleven domes, each representing one of India's more notable edifices. Its ground-floor stalls are laden with herbs, curries and culinary products; on the floor above are more conventional shops and a number of enticing eateries; there is a walkway leadng to the fresh fish market. The market has basement parking, and is open Monday to Saturday 06h00 to 18h00, and Sunday 10h00 to 16h00.

Art Gallery

Founded in 1892 and housed in the City Hall (use the Smith Street entrance directly opposite The Playhouse theatre), Durban's Art Gallery offers a fairly impressive permanent collection of European works, including a selection of paintings by Constable, Utrillo, Corot and Lely, sculptures by Rodin and Dalau, glassware by Lalique; French and Chinese ceramics and numerous objets d'art. However, in recent years the collecting emphasis has shifted onto the local scene, and on view are some fine examples of South African art and applied art, together with an especially eye-catching selection of KwaZulu-Natal craftwork in which intricate Zulu beadwork and basketry feature prominently. Open Monday to Saturday from 08h30 to 17h00 (Thursdays till 19h00), Sundays from 11h00 to 17h00. Guided tours are also available; tel. 300-6238.

Natural Science Museum

Located in the City Hall, this museum serves as an invaluable introduction to South Africa's wildlife heritage. On show are fine displays of animal, bird and reptile life, fishes, invertebrates, together with a geological section. Among the more intriguing of the exhibits is a model of *Tyrannosaurus rex*, most fearsome of the dinosaurs, a 2 300-year-old Egyptian mummy, and the skeleton of the proverbial dodo, the large ground-living bird that inhabited the islands of the Indian Ocean until early sea-farers hunted them to extinction (the last specimen was recorded in 1680 on the island of Mauritius). Special sections are devoted to an electronic 'Journey through Time' experience, and to a multi-media computer centre called KwaZuzulwazi, or 'place of discovery', where you can explore the wonders of the natural world through both personal participation and CD-Rom. Open Monday to Saturday 08h30 to 17h00, Sundays and public holidays 11h00 to 17h00; no admission charged. Guided tours are offered; tel. 300-6212.

Durban's grand late-Victorian City Hall.

 TOURIST JUNCTION

*When visiting Durban, make Tourist Junction your first port of call. At this one-stop tourist information centre (on the first floor of the grand old station building at 160 Pine Street), **Durban Unlimited** will sort out your hotel, tour and Natal Parks Board bookings, provide information on attractions and much more. There is a curio shop and restaurant on the premises, and guided city walks are also offered. Tourist Junction is open Monday to Friday 08h00 to 17h00; Saturday and Sunday 09h00 to 14h00; tel. 304-4934. For the after-hours Teletourist Service; tel. 305-3877 (English), or 305-2723 (Zulu).*

DURBAN EXPERIENCE

This guided walk, on Tuesdays, introduces you to part of Durban's cultural scene. Ports of call on the itinerary include the Play-house theatre complex, the Local History Museum and the City Hall. Bookings can be made through Durban Unlimited (see p 62).

HISTORICAL WALKABOUT

This is one of three guided morning walks which are organized by and bookable through Durban Unlimited (see p 62). The route embraces Durban's first railway station (the inaugural 3.2-km (2-mile) line, South Africa's first, opened in 1860 to link the town centre with The Point) and its later conversion, the Francis Farewell Gardens, the Local History Museum and various points of interest along the popular Victoria Embankment.

The Playhouse

Focal point of the city's performing arts scene, the five-auditorium Playhouse in Smith Street, opposite the City Hall, merits a visit not only for the lively and highly professional shows it stages but also for its history and décor. For years the complex functioned as two grand cinemas, each of them a well-loved city landmark – the Tudor-style Playhouse and the mock-Moorish Princes (renamed the Colosseum), silver-screen meccas that later hosted a succession of luminaries from the live arts and entertainment world, among them Richard Tauber, Noel Coward and Maurice Chevalier. After a time of much-needed renovations, the new Playhouse opened in 1986 as a stylish state-of-the-art quintet of venues, though some features of the old picture palaces – notably the exotic façade, the foyers, the original star-spangled ceiling and the interior 'battlements' – have been retained. The busy calendar includes ballet, opera, orchestral music presented by the Natal Philharmonic, recitals, straight and experimental drama, intimate supper theatre, art and other exhibitions. Consult the local newspapers for what's-on details. Tours are conducted on Tuesdays; tel. 304-3631.

The idiosyncratic Playhouse, hub of the city's vibrant arts scene.

Clay pots are popular Durban artefacts.

Local History Museum

Located in the Old Court House, Aliwal Street (between West and Smith streets), this museum features the region's multi-cultural (but largely colonial) heritage in a series of permanent thematic displays and temporary exhibitions. Notable among the former are the clothes and accessories of the costume section, and the collection of figurines representing a virtual who's who of past leaders in various fields. Upstairs is the Durban Room, with its various evocative reconstructions – of an early settler's cottage, an apothecary, a sugar mill – and the 'fancy repository' of period jewellery, porcelain, toys and so on. Among the museum's satellites are the Maritime Museum (*see* p 29), the Old House Museum (*see* p 26), and the Kwa Muhle Museum at 130–132 Ordinance Road, where the focus is on 20th-century Durban and its people. The Local History Museum is open Monday to Saturday 08h30 to 17h00, Sundays and public holidays 11h00 to 17h00; no admission charged. Guided tours are available by appointment; tel. 300-6244.

ARTS-AND-CRAFTS MEANDERS

*Notable among these is the **Berea Artists at Home,** an itinerary which embraces a number of local studios and workshops that, between them, turn out work ranging from painting, sculpture and ceramics to stained glass, marbling and quilting.*
*Others include the **Durban North Meander,** on the last Sunday of each month, and the complementary **Umhlanga Arts-and-Crafts Market.***
*Further afield are the **Shongololo Crawl,** which takes in the Amanzimtoti area, the **South Coast Wildabout** and the celebrated **Midlands Meander,** involving a pleasant drive around the countryside to the north of Pietermaritzburg (see p 49).*
Contact Durban Unlimited for maps and further details.

AGFA
PHOTO TIP

Most international film brands are readily available from photographic shops, pharmacies and department stores. Processing is quick (one hour at some outlets). Enquire whether process charges are included in the price of the film.

Zulu beadwork is encoded with meanings.

The African Art Centre

This non-profit enterprise in the Guildhall Arcade off Gardiner Street (between Smith Street and Victoria Embankment), initiated as a self-help project, functions as part-gallery part-shop and is well worth a visit. On display is an interesting collection of graphic art and sculptures as well as an array of pleasing fabrics, pottery, Zulu beadwork, basketry, woodwork and African rugs crafted at the renowned Rourke's Drift centre. The centre is open Monday to Thursday 08h30 to 17h00, Friday 07h30 to 16h00, and Saturday 08h30 to 12h30.

FASHIONS OF THE FOREFATHERS

The lovely beadwork that adorns the traditional Zulu is a relatively recent feature: the beads were introduced by 19th-century white traders. They have, though, assumed an enchanting significance. Stitched together in intricately ornamental designs, their colours convey subtle messages – of love, loyalty, happiness, sadness and so forth.

Before the advent of modern fabrics, the Zulu warrior's clothing comprised hides and pelts embellished in various ways to distinguish the age-graded regiments. The 'uniform' was completed by plumes and patterned ox-hide shields.

The Workshop

Durban's cavernous Victorian railways workshop in Aliwal Street has been transformed into a showpiece for shoppers. It incorporates more than 120 speciality outlets, many designed in charming Natal-colonial style, the décor an appealing mélange of wrought ironwork, coloured fanlights and brass trimmings. Here you'll find Victorian-type barrow stalls crammed with wares both functional and fanciful, as well as an inviting variety of eateries, pubs, bistros and buskers. Open seven days a week; there's plenty of underground parking.

The Workshop, a shopaholic's paradise.

Sea World

Ranked among the southern hemisphere's finest marine-life complexes, Sea World Aquarium and Dolphinarium (at the ocean end of West Street) embraces a fantasia of tropical fish together with sharks, sting-rays, giant leatherback and loggerhead turtles, octopuses, crustaceans, corals, colourful anemones and seashells. Scuba-divers enter the massive main tank to feed the inmates by hand (the sharks are fed at 12h30 on Tuesdays, Thursdays and Sundays), and next door, at the Dolphinarium, not only dolphins but also seals and Cape jackass penguins entertain visitors.

Your entrance fee helps support the less obvious, more serious side of Sea World: the place functions as a respected research centre that numbers dolphin, seal and penguin breeding programmes among its successful projects. It also rescues, treats and rehabilitates injured marine mammals and birds. Open daily 09h00 to 21h00. To confirm show times; tel. 37-4079.

i **TOURIST INFORMATION**

Visitors and beachgoers in search of information on tours, events, accommodation and attractions in the Durban and surrounding areas have the convenient option of using a tourist information office right on the beachfront (adjacent to Sea World, Marine Parade). The office is open from Monday to Friday 08h00 to 16h30, Saturday 08h30 to 16h30 and Sunday 09h00 to 16h00; tel. 32-2595 for further information.

The most sociable of Sea World's guests are its dolphins.

Amphitheatre

Those in need of a break from the hustle and bustle of the city can retreat to the Amphitheatre, an enticingly restful sunken garden of emerald lawn, bright flowers, cool fountains and pools, footbridges and an open-air auditorium.

The gardens are located opposite the Crowne Plaza Holiday Inn, just beyond North Beach. Each Sunday a fleamarket is held here, offering anything from arts and crafts to refreshments and entertainment for children. There's plenty of parking, and its proximity to the beachfront makes it an ideal family outing.

Rides by Ricksha

Among Durban's more distinctive features are the rickshas that ply along the seafront. Parked near the Amphitheatre on Marine Parade, these lightly built, man-pulled, highly colourful carts were introduced from Japan (they were originally known as 'jinrikishas') during the 1890s to provide a functional taxi service, and proved so popular that by 1904 there were more than 2 000 of them on the streets.

The first models were plain-looking enough, but with increasing competition from motorized transport they became far more ornate, both the carriage and its Zulu 'driver' elaborately decorated with beads, furs and colourful streamers. They have survived the years, but only as a tourist attraction.

The quiet Japanese Gardens.

Minitown

This is a delightful drawcard for both the young and the young-at-heart. Superbly crafted, this beachfront miniature city (located at the ocean end of Somtsue Street, off Snell Parade), modelled on Amsterdam's celebrated Madurodam,

The ornate rickshas are distinctive of Durban, though they originally came from Japan.

OPEN-AIR SHOPPING

Street and craft markets are an animated feature of the Durban scene. Among leading venues are the:

Amphitheatre, *North Beach; every Sunday (see p 20).*

Berea Fleamarket, *Essenwood Road; every Saturday, 09h00 to 14h00.*

Bluff Fleamarket, *Showgrounds; first and last Saturday of each month, 09h00 to 15h00.*

Church Street Arts & Crafts, *next to the Church Street post office; open seven days a week, 08h30 to 16h00.*

Durban Antique Fair, *outside the Royal Hotel; last Sunday of each month, 09h30 to 16h00.*

Farepark Market, *between West and Pine streets; open seven days a week 09h00 to 17h00 (Saturdays 09h00 to 21h00).*

South Plaza Market, *Exhibition Centre; every Sunday, 09h00 to 16h00.*

Minitown is perfectly to scale.

 AGFA

PHOTO TIP

*When you pay a visit to Durban's delightful miniature city, **Minitown**, be sure to have a camera handy as there are plenty of opportunities for fun photos.*

features Durban's harbour and its shipping, lilliputian thoroughfares and their diminutive traffic, together with some of the city's more prominent buildings, such as the City Hall, as well as several shopping malls, hotels and so forth – all meticulously constructed (by local amateur modellers) to a scale of 1:25. It also has a mini-airport, railway complex and a number of landmarks drawn from the cities of Johannesburg and Cape Town. In the evening visitors have the added attractions of a funfair. Minitown is open from Tuesday to Saturday 09h30 to 20h00, and Sunday 09h30 to 17h00.

Fitzsimons Snake Park

A fascinating selection of southern Africa's nearly 165 types of snake is on view in this well-conceived and visitor-friendly reptile centre, together with quite a large number of exotic species (their cage temperatures are thermostatically controlled), crocodiles, leguaans, tortoises, terrapins and turtles.

About 10 per cent of the region's snakes are classed as highly poisonous – venomous enough to inflict a fatal bite – among them the mambas (several kinds are in residence here), cobras, adders, and the tree-dwelling boomslang (*see* right).

Located at 240A Lower Marine Parade, Fitzsimons also serves as a rehabilitation centre for reptiles, and has a curio shop. Demonstrations for the public are held daily, throughout the year, at 10h00, 11h30, 13h00, 14h30 and 15h30; the snakes are fed on Saturdays and Sundays after each demonstration; the crocs each day at 14h00 during the warmer months. The park is open seven days a week 09h00 to 17h00 (till 16h30 out of season). To confirm show times; tel. 37-6456.

The lethal boomslang.

THE WHEEL

Durban is noted for its splendid shopping complexes, but for eye-catching décor and sheer exuberance few compare with The Wheel in Gillespie Street, close to South Beach. The place derives its name from the giant revolving Ferris wheel that dominates its façade; inside are well over a hundred speciality shops, 12 cinemas, restaurants, a 'mothers' room', basketball court and entertainment in Funland and the Zone 4 Laser Centre. The general theme is nautical: ships' decking, railings, spars, lifeboats and flags decorate the open areas. There is ample under-roof parking; open seven days a week, 09h00 till late.

The Wheel caters for shoppers and nonshoppers alike.

AGFA

PHOTO TIP

*For ever-changing and magnificent vistas of the city and harbour, make a point of lunching at **Roma Revolving Restaurant** (Italian) on the 30th floor of John Ross House, Jonsson Road. The restaurant constantly (and very slowly) moves through 360 degrees, providing some of the best panoramas of the city. It is open for lunch and dinner; tel. 37-6707 to make a reservation.*

VICTORIA EMBANKMENT

The Embankment (or Esplanade) running along Durban Harbour's north-western shore beckons the bayside stroller with its waterfront views and historical buildings, among which are the colonial-style Old Supreme Court and the Durban Club, built during the Edwardian era. Special points of interest along the Victoria Embankment are covered in more detail below.

John Ross Statue

Start your journey of discovery at the eastern end of the Embankment where you will find the bronze statue honouring one of Durban's courageous hero's – 15-year-old John Ross, who in 1826 walked the 700 or so kilometres (435 miles) to Delagoa Bay (today known as Maputo) in quest of medical supplies for Durban's first, ailing settler community.

Durban is a favourite with the yachting fraternity.

More than just a pretty face: Vasco da Gama Clock has historic value.

Vasco da Gama Clock

Among the Victoria Embankment's more familiar features is the Vasco da Gama Clock, presented by the Portuguese government in 1897 to commemorate the navigator's pioneering voyage 400 years before. Mounted on a colourfully intricate cast-iron dome-shaped gazebo, this four-faced clock is a fine example of Victorian baroque work.

Dick King Statue

The equestrian statue of Dick King, hero of the short, sharp confrontation between British troops and the newly arrived Voortrekkers in 1842, can be seen in the gardens at the harbour end of Gardiner Street. Charged by the commander of the besieged British garrison to deliver dispatches to, and seek reinforcements from, distant Grahamstown, King and his Zulu helpmeet, Ndongeni, set out on the gruelling 960-km (597-mile) ride through hostile territory. King, parting company with Ndongeni in Pondoland, completed the epic journey in just ten days. The Old Fort, where the siege took place, is in Old Fort Road (*see* p 15).

ALBERT PARK
Located at the western end of the Victoria Embankment, this green oasis not only is a welcome resting place for the footsore sightseer but is also ideal for the more energetic visitor, with walks, jogging routes and exercise stations conveniently close to the city centre. The park also has an alfresco restaurant – a popular lunchtime venue – and a giant open-air chessboard.

LADY IN WHITE
A statue marks the place where Perla Siedle Gibson, the matronly and much-loved 'Lady in White', stood to sing to the Allied servicemen aboard the troopships entering and leaving the harbour during WW I. The statue, unveiled by Queen Elizabeth II on her visit in 1995, stands next to the Ocean Terminal Building.

A SAD SAGA
The prime mover in the founding of Durban was Capt Allen Gardiner, a retired naval officer and missionary who in 1834, after rejection by the Zulu monarch Dingane, was welcomed by the resident whites and built a mission station on the slopes overlooking the harbour. This he named Berea, a reference to St Paul, who came to Berea (in Macedonia) where the people 'received the Word with all readiness of mind'. His remaining years were full of disappointment and, ultimately, tragedy. He failed to have British authority extended over the region and left Natal in 1838. He died, in 1851, of starvation in the bleakness of Tierra del Fuego at the southern tip of South America.

Old House Museum

Once the home of Sir John Robinson, Natal's first prime minister, The Old House (31 St Andrews Street) has been beautifully restored and furnished in Victorian style to serve as a reminder of Durban's colonial heritage. This charming settler's home features a collection of domestic items, furniture, paintings of Durban in its heyday and, perhaps most noteworthy of all, an early French clock – a remarkable time-piece that also tells you the day, the phases of the moon, the air pressure and much else. The museum is open Monday to Saturday 08h30 to 17h00, Sunday and public holidays 11h00 to 17h00. There is no admission charge.

THE HARBOUR

The city of Durban's spacious 1 668-ha (4 122-acre) bay is the setting for Africa's premier and the world's ninth-biggest and busiest harbour, a vast concourse of quays, cranes, trains, warehouses, pre-cooling stores, huge grain elevators, silos and other installations through which tens of millions of tons of cargo – sugar and subtropical fruits, maize, manganese, coal, oil, a variety of manufactured goods and much else – pass each year.

The Portuguese navigator Vasco da Gama was the very first European to visit the Bay – around Christmastide in 1497 (hence the name 'Natal'), on his epic route-charting voyage to India – but more than three centuries elapsed before white men began to make a permanent home among the Nguni people.

In 1824 a small party of white hunters and traders came ashore to treat with the great warrior-king Shaka Zulu and to open up a profitable traffic in ivory and skins. Their rudimentary bayshore settlement grew to become South Africa's third-largest city, but the harbour was slow to develop: the Bay is almost completely landlocked, its southern waters bounded by an 8-km-long (5-mile), 2 250-m-high (7 400-ft) wooded headland called The Bluff (see p 32), and its northern waters by a narrower, lower-lying spit known as The Point, and for decades passage through the narrow entrance was constantly bedevilled by a shifting sandbar. During most of the 19th century the low-water depth at the mouth of the harbour hovered around the 2-m (6-ft) mark, but intensive dredging and

AGFA
PHOTO TIP

North Pier, along the Point, provides excellent opportunities for early-morning and sunset photographs of Durban's highrise buildings and golden beachfront.

The view of Durban's city centre from the harbour.

The Victoria Embankment's small craft harbour.

Harbour cruises are part of the Durban experience, with ample opportunities for photographs. On offer are:
Durban Ferry Services, day and night cruises on the hour departing from the jetty next to the Maritime Museum; tel. 361-8727.
Sarie Marais, deep-sea and harbour cruises (15h00 and 11h00), departing from Gardiner Street Jetty; booking essential; tel. 305-4022.
Meridian Sailing School, harbour cruises; day trips off-shore; voyages to Cape Town, Maputo or Madagascar. For more details call at 7 Fenton Road (3-minute walk from yacht harbour); tel. 304-1500.

sand-pumping eventually cleared the way, and on the 26th of June 1892 the first ocean-going liner sailed in. Visitors can explore the harbour area by car, or on foot, or by boat, aboard the functional round-the-bay ferry or on one of the sight-seeing cruises on offer.

Besides the sugar terminals and the Maritime Museum (which are covered in more detail below), the Prince Edward graving dock – the southern hemisphere's largest dry-dock – and the nearby floating dock are also sights worth seeing when ships are in for repair.

The Point has been earmarked for a tourist development scheme that, it is said, will eventually rival Cape Town's Waterfront in both scope and imagination.

Sugar Terminals

Girding the western end of the harbour is Maydon Wharf, with its sugar terminals and grain elevators and, towards the city end, its busy deep-sea fishing berths. The three sugar silos (at 57 Maydon Road) are especially impressive: enormous 300-m-long (1 000-ft) buildings whose award-winning design has set international standards and which, together, can accommodate more than half a million tons of the commodity. On arrival from the plantations the raw sugar is mechanically poured from above in sudden avalanches that pile up in mountainous dunes of sweetness, and is then siphoned (at the rate of 1 000 tons an hour) through an elaborate system of hoppers, weighing machines and conveyor belts to be loaded onto the waiting ship.

You can view the spectacular process on one of the guided tours conducted on Mondays to Thursdays at 09h00, 11h00 and 14h00, and Fridays at 09h00 and 11h00. To confirm tour times; tel. 301-0331.

Maritime Museum

The museum provides an intriguing insight into the city's seafaring past, but without the usual exhibition halls and glass cases. Its displays are multi-ton affairs, chief among which is the classic steam-tug *JR More*, the last of its kind to be built and the world's only survivor of the powerful twin-screw models. There are also the naval minesweeper *SAS Durban,* the early (1927) pilot boat *Ulundi,* and Sea View Cottage, a re-created early settler home. Visitor amenities include a gift shop, video presentations and, for children, a 'Pirate Experience'. The museum is located at the harbour end of Aliwal Street and is open Monday to Saturday 08h30 to 16h00, Sunday 11h00 to 16h00.

 VINTAGE JOURNEY
For a sightseeing trip with a difference, book your place on the Umgeni Steam Train that puffs its way up the old main line between Kloof and Inchanga just to the west of the city. Three excursions set out on the last Sunday of each month; other runs depart from The Point during holiday periods.

The Railway was launched in the early 1980s with just a single engine and coach; today it is the proud owner of 20 locomotives and more than 60 coaches. Many of its historic treasures can be seen at the Railway Museum at Hilton (see p 43).

The Maritime Museum's JR More *steam-tug.*

OUTER DURBAN

GAME-VIEWING DRIVES

Enjoy a bush experience at the Kenneth Stainbank reserve, only minutes away from the city centre, where the Natal Parks Board offers night game-viewing drives under the guidance of qualified rangers. For further information; tel. 469-2807.

AGFA *agfa*
PHOTO TIP

The University of Natal campus, on Berea ridge, provides superb views and wonderful photographic opportunities of Durban, its golden beaches and the Indian Ocean in the distance. The easiest way there is to take the Howard College Bus from the Pine Street bus terminal.

There's a wealth of sightseeing interest within easy driving distance of central Durban. The suburbs are graced by some lovely parks, each with its distinctive place in the environmental scheme; the neighbouring coastal centres, both to the north and south, offer sun, sea, sand and much else; inland is the scenic grandeur of the Umgeni Valley and its Thousand Hills.

YELLOWWOOD PARK

This residential suburb lies 10 km (6 miles) south-west of the city centre. Follow the Old South Coast Road (M3) from the city and turn into Kenyon Howden Road. Once in Yellowwood Park, the road to the Kenneth Stainbank Nature Reserve is well signposted.

Kenneth Stainbank Nature Reserve

Donated to the Natal Parks Board by the Stainbank family, this sanctuary protects the precious flora – grassland and coastal forest – that covers the lower reaches of the Little Mhlatuzana River that discharges into the southern part of Durban Harbour. It also nurtures an impressive array of wildlife, including zebra, bushbuck, impala, blue, grey and red duiker and reedbuck. The bird life is also worth a mention – more than 150 species have been identified.

Self-guided trails (including a specially designed trail for people in wheelchairs) and night game-viewing drives enable visitors to experience the 'real Africa' within shouting distance of central Durban; picnic spots envite you to linger. Maps and bird and animal lists are available at the entrance, and there is a curio shop that also serves refreshments. Visitors are advised to use insect repellents as ticks can be troublesome. The reserve is open during daylight hours throughout the year.

A nature trail for everyone at Kenneth Stainbank.

as breeding grounds for certain species of fish, crab and mollusc, and providing a protective barrier against the fierce tropical storms that threaten the estuarine systems.

Of the earth's 660 or so species of mangrove, eight are indigenous to the KwaZulu-Natal shoreline, but few patches have survived the encroachment of man, so the Beachwood Mangroves reserve ranks high among the region's conservancies.

Located on the northern bank of the Umgeni River mouth, the reserve has a bird-watching hide, picnic sites, nature trails and caravan and camp sites. Day visitors are welcome, and should use the Rocket Hut entrance, off Fairway Road. The reserve is open daily 05h00 to 22h00. Guided tours may be arranged through the Natal Parks Board; tel. 84-0818 or 25-1271.

> **i** **MUDHOPPER**
> Unique to the region's mangroves is this amphibious fish that uses its fins to propel itself along the surface of the water and on land. When submerged, it breathes through its gills, but uses a different respiratory system for terrestial living, taking in oxygenated water through its mouth for storage in its gills. It also absorbs air through its skin.

Umhlanga Rocks: jewel of the Dolphin Coast.

UMHLANGA ROCKS

This fashionable seaside resort, on the sunlit Dolphin Coast beyond the Umgeni River 18 km (11 miles) north of the city (take the M4 Northern Freeway), is small enough to be classed as a village but it embraces almost as wide a range of amenities and attractions as Durban itself – stylish hotels, gleaming apartment complexes, shopping centres, a multiplicity of restaurants, a tranquil lagoon and golden stretches of sand.

> **AGFA**
> **PHOTO TIP**
> A stroll along the 3-km (1.9-mile) promenade to **Umhlanga's lighthouse** offers vistas of the ocean and opportunities for early morning or sunset photos.

The regal African fish eagle.

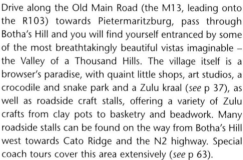

Umhlanga Lagoon Nature Reserve

Worth a morning of your time is this reserve, whose waters and dune forest (red milkwood is a prominent resident) attract a large number and variety of birds, among them the imperious African fish eagle. The reserve is open daily from 06h00 to 18h00, has picnic sites and can be explored at leisure along the established nature trails. The entrance gate is just past the Breakers Resort Hotel in Lagoon Drive.

WORLD OF SHARKS
Southern Africa's waters are home to 109 known kinds of shark, of which 10 are dangerous to man. Among the more common are the grotesque-looking hammerhead, the blue shark and the great white shark. This last is known as the 'white death' and can grow to over 6 m (20 ft) in length.

From Tuesday to Thursday, and on the first Sunday of each month, the Natal Sharks Board entertains visitors to its headquarters in Umhlanga Rocks Drive with informative shows, including audio-visual presentations and dissecting demonstrations. It is prudent to book in advance; tel. 561-1001.

BOTHA'S HILL AND ENVIRONS

Drive along the Old Main Road (the M13, leading onto the R103) towards Pietermaritzburg, pass through Botha's Hill and you will find yourself entranced by some of the most breathtakingly beautiful vistas imaginable – the Valley of a Thousand Hills. The village itself is a browser's paradise, with quaint little shops, art studios, a crocodile and snake park and a Zulu kraal (*see* p 37), as well as roadside craft stalls, offering a variety of Zulu crafts from clay pots to basketry and beadwork. Many roadside stalls can be found on the way from Botha's Hill west towards Cato Ridge and the N2 highway. Special coach tours cover this area extensively (*see* p 63).

Valley of a Thousand Hills
Stretching from the distinctively flat-topped, 960-m-high (3 200-ft) massif known as Natal Table Mountain, near Pietermaritzburg, to the Indian Ocean coastline 65 km (40 miles) to the east, is the Valley of a Thousand Hills. The uplands are densely populated in parts, but much of the area remains a ruggedly unspoilt wilderness of peak, plateau, wooded slope, deep ravine and natural garden famed for the luxuriance of its wild flowers – arum and fire lilies, crimson aloes, dramatic red-hot pokers and many others.

PheZulu

PheZulu (meaning 'high-up'), located on Old Main Road, a stone's throw from both the Rob Roy Hotel and the Assagay Safari Park, features Zulu dancing to the powerful beat of drums and also displays of African domestic routines and crafts – cooking, brewing, thatching, beading, spear-making and so forth. PheZulu's sangoma throws bones for the benefit of visitors; its shop sells wood-carvings, pottery, beadwork and basketware. There is an art gallery, and a tea garden overlooking the Valley of a Thousand Hills. Open daily 09h00 to 16h30; Zulu dancing at 10h00, 11h30, 13h30 and 15h30. Guided tours are offered; tel 777-1000. Entrance fees includes a visit to Assagay Safari Park.

Assagay Safari Park

Like PheZulu, this park is a prime tourist drawcard, featuring over a hundred crocodiles lounging in ponds, a crocodile museum, and a restaurant serving crocodile steaks as its speciality. Adjoining the crocodile ponds is a snake park, a curio shop, and picnic and barbecue sites offering lovely views of the Valley of a Thousand Hills. Open seven days a week 09h00 to 16h30.

 WAYS OF THE SANGOMA

The Zulu sangoma, commonly but incorrectly referred to as a 'witch-doctor', is a spirit medium (and diviner) who acts as intermediary between the ancestors and their living descendants, and is able to diagnose and predict all kinds of ills, especially those of a psychological and social nature. A sangoma is recruited through a mystical process, by the ancestors, and undergoes long, rigorous training under the tutelage of an experienced diviner. Visit sangomas at PheZulu, Shakaland and DumaZulu (see p 54).

Traditional Zulu villages feature memorable Zulu dancing, such as this at Shakaland (see p 54).

EXCURSIONS

i **SARDINE RUN**
Each winter, shoals
of migrating sardines come
close inshore to provide a
remarkable spectacle – the
sea literally churns with their
passage. Sometimes weather
conditions and the atten-
dant predators – sea-birds,
barracudas and other game
fish – drive the sardines into
the surf itself, whereupon
hundreds of bystanders
wade into waves to scoop
them into buckets and nets.

Durban itself offers a fine array of attractions, but it will also serve as a convenient base from which to explore a wider region equally endowed with tourist drawcards. Recommended destinations include the resort centres of the magnificent shoreline, the charming inland city of Pietermaritzburg, the foothills of the awesome Drakensberg range to the west, and the renowned wildlife sanctuaries of northern KwaZulu-Natal.

THE SOUTH COAST

The coastline running south from Durban to the Eastern Cape border ranks among the most popular, and most beautiful, of the southern hemisphere's holiday regions, one that numbers among its assets a balmy climate, the warm and welcoming waters of the Indian Ocean, superb stretches of sand, a score and more charming

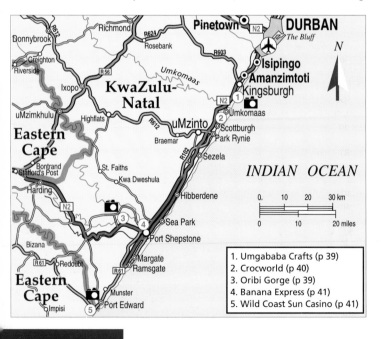

1. Umgababa Crafts (p 39)
2. Crocworld (p 40)
3. Oribi Gorge (p 39)
4. Banana Express (p 41)
5. Wild Coast Sun Casino (p 41)

Impressive Oribi Gorge, named after the region's graceful oribi buck.

river estuaries and lagoons, a lush hinterland and a chain of pretty little towns, villages and hamlets that beckon the leisure-bent visitor with their full range of accommodation and recreational facilities.

Special points of interest – Oribi Gorge, the Wild Coast Sun, the Banana Express, and Scottburgh's Crocworld – along the coastline are discussed in more detail below.

PORT SHEPSTONE
Situated on the N2, 122 km (76 miles) south of Durban, this coastal town numbers among its attractions the nearby Oribi Gorge and the delightful Banana Express steam-train (*see* p 41).

 Oribi Gorge
This spectacular 24-km-long (15-mile) canyon carved from the sandstone terrain by the Umzimkulwana River, is located about 20 km (12½ miles) inland from Port Shepstone. The Oribi Gorge, more than 350 m (1 165 ft) deep in places, is the centrepiece of a splendid nature reserve noted for its rugged hills and precipitous

 ROADSIDE CRAFTS
On your drive down the scenic South Coast, make a point of stopping at Umgababa. Here, traders invite you to browse among stalls laden with Zulu crafts, tropical fruits and much else.

AGFA *Agfa*
PHOTO TIP
*Among the best South Coast vantage points is Hanging Rock, an outcrop overlooking **Oribi Gorge**. Here, the camera captures unforgettable vistas. Other spots are Horseshoe Bend, Baboon's Castle and the Pulpit.*

CROCS ON DISPLAY

Crocworld, about 4 km (2½ miles) outside Scottburgh, is well worth visiting for its 10 000 or so giant reptiles, its wildlife museum, snake pit, nature trails, prolific bird life and lovely gardens.

Guided tours include a video show of what is claimed to be the finest footage ever shot of crocodiles on the hunt.

The complex also embraces a meticulously re-created 19th-century Zulu village, with traditional dancing displays at 14h00 daily (except Mondays). Crocworld is open daily, 08h00 to 16h30 (17h00 in season).

A croc-mom carries her young in her mouth.

valleys, its forests, perennial streams and waterfalls. It is also home to some 40 species of mammal – chacma baboons, samango monkeys and various antelope, including the graceful oribi buck that gave its name to the sanctuary. Here you'll also find an impressive 260 different kinds of bird.

Among visitor amenities are several nature trails, picnic and fishing spots, a hutted camp run by the Natal Parks Board; tel. (0331) 47-1981; and the privately owned Oribi Gorge Hotel; tel. (0397) 9-1753.

PORT EDWARD

This lively resort town, 172 km (107 miles) from Durban, is the last stop along the coastal road before you cross the provincial border to one of South Africa's foremost hotel-casino complexes, the Wild Coast Sun.

AGFA
PHOTO TIP

*You will capture some fine scenic shots from the CH Mitchell bridge that crosses the **Umtamvuna River** between Port Edward and the Wild Coast Sun.*

Upstream are rank upon rank of densely forested cliffs; downstream the lens takes in sweeping beach and ocean, both decorated by a multitude of attractively colourful leisure craft.

Chacma baboons are easily seen at Oribi Gorge.

Wild Coast Sun

Reminiscent – in both its design and general surrounds – of a tropically enchanting South Sea Island venue, the resort is set beside a tranquil lagoon on the northernmost segment of the stunning Eastern Cape seaboard. On offer are gaming rooms, restaurants, cocktail and show bars; an 18-hole golf course that ranks among the country's finest; tennis and squash courts; bowling greens; sea-angling spots that yield excellent catches; and sailing, canoeing and water-skiing at Waterworld. The beautifully landscaped grounds invite strollers; more energetic walkers are drawn to the rocky headlands and wide beaches of the shoreline and the hills of the hinterland.

A regular coach service plies between central Durban and the Wild Coast Sun; contact Durban Unlimited for more details (*see* p 62). Accommodation bookings: Sun International central reservations; tel. (011) 780-7800.

BANANA EXPRESS

Not to be missed is a journey on this vintage steam train that makes its leisurely, narrow-gauge way from Port Shepstone to Paddock twice a week. The superb scenery and journey evoke a less hurried, more romantic era. On offer are full-day (or shorter) trips, including excursions to Oribi Gorge where you'll be treated to a barbecue and a ramble along the Baboon View Walk. Booking essential; tel. (03931) 7-6443.

You'll find a room with a view aboard the Banana Express.

i **PUBLICITY HOUSE**

The local tourist information bureau can be found on the corner of Commercial Road and Longmarket Street; tel. (0331) 5-3318. The building, completed in 1884, is now a national monument.

 CITY HALL

Pietermaritzburg's City Hall, completed in 1893 on the site of the old Volks-raadsaal (the Voortrekker parliament), is reputedly the largest red-brick building in the southern hemisphere. Especially notable features are its domes, its fine stained-glass windows, its clock tower, which rises a full 47 m (154 ft) from the pavement below, and its pipe organ, a splendid affair built in 1901 and later modernized, complete with a mobile console.

PIETERMARITZBURG & ENVIRONS

On the misty uplands some 90 km (55 miles) inland from Durban is Pietermaritzburg, the historic provincial capital (though that status is being challenged by Ulundi, far to the north) and a charming little city renowned for its red-brick Victorian buildings, and for the roses and azaleas that bloom in its lovely parks.

1. Voortrekker Museum (p 42)
2. City Hall (p 42)
3. Tatham Art Gallery (p 43)
4. Natal Museum (p 43)

5. Alexandra Park (p 44)
6. Macrorie House (p 43)
7. Botanic Gardens (p 45)
8. Queen Elizabeth Park (p 45)
9. Worlds View (p 42)

MUSEUMS, GALLERIES AND LANDMARKS

Much of the city's Voortrekker and colonial legacy has been preserved in its magnificent buildings, museums and landmarks – indeed so much survives from the past that the place is often referred to as 'the Heritage City'. Among the highligts are:

 Voortrekker Museum

This museum in Church Street was built in 1841 as the Church of the Vow to commemorate the Boer-Zulu confrontation at Blood River in 1938: shortly before the battle the Voortrekkers promised that should the Almighty grant them victory, they would dedicate their place of worship as a memorial for future generations. Inside, you'll find an intriguing collection of relics, including a Trekker ox-wagon and a wooden chair carved by Zulu headmen for their paramount chief Dingane. Entry is free of charge; open Monday to Friday 09h00 to 16h00 and Saturday 08h00 to 12h00.

Tatham Art Gallery

Also well worth a visit is this art gallery in Commercial Road, an elegant red-brick building that began life in 1871 as the Supreme Court. On display are fine examples of Zulu art and crafts and works by leading local painters together with an impressive selection of European masterpieces. The gallery is open every day (except Monday) 10h00 to 18h00.

After that, take a stroll up nearby Churchill Mall to view the **Gandhi Statue**, erected in 1993 to commemorate Mahatma Gandhi's arrival in Natal a century before.

Macrorie House

Reminders of bygone days can be seen in Macrorie House (corner of Loop and Pine streets), a Victorian period museum containing early furnishings and ornamentation. Open Monday, Wednesday and Thursday 09h00 to 13h00 and Sunday 09h00 to 17h00.

Natal Museum

Another must for browsers is the Natal Museum, whose widely-varied exhibits include a delightful cluster of 1850s houses and shops (natural history and ethnology also feature). Open Monday to Saturday 09h00 to 16h30 and Sunday 14h00 to 17h00.

PARKS AND GARDENS

Pietermaritzburg is also known, informally, as the 'City of Flowers' – and deservedly so. Much of this floral glory can be seen and enjoyed along the **Green Belt Trails** that wind their way through suburb and surrounds. Details and a comprehensive map are available from the publicity association.

 ON-LINE SHOW
*Railway enthusiasts should beat a path to the **Natal Railway Museum** at Hilton, just to the northwest of Pietermaritzburg. On display is rolling stock of the 1930s period; notable are the bullion and engineers' coaches, the sleeper coach (which dates from 1903) and the dining and kitchen cars, together with a dozen vintage locomotives. The museum is operated by the all-volunteer Umgeni Steam Railway enterprise, which lays on guided tours and sightseeing excursions along the old main line between Kloof and Nchanga to the west of Durban. Trips set out on the second Sunday of each month and on selected public holidays. The museum is open daily 08h00-16h00; tel. (0331) 43-1857.*

Pietermaritzburg's City Hall at night.

Alexandra Park's gracious Victorian bandstand.

 Alexandra Park

This attractive park with its pagoda-like pavilion and cricket oval, charming 1892 bandstand, neat flower gardens and pleasant picnic spots, is only a stone's throw from the city centre, via either Commercial or College road.

 AGFA
PHOTO TIP

*The Natal Midlands is renowned for its waterfalls, the highest of which are the splendid **Karkloof** at 105 m (345 ft). Other waterfalls worth visiting are:*

** The **Albert Falls**, on the Greytown road: the cascades are modest enough but the surrounding countryside, occupied by lake and nature reserve, is enchanting.*

** The much-photographed **Howick Falls**, which plunge 95 m (310 ft) into the Umgeni River. Again, the immediate surroundings are magical in their beauty. Close by is the popular **Midmar** resort and its nature reserve, its large dam (much favoured for water sports), its Zulu homestead and 'historical village'.*

Cascading Howick Falls plunge into the Umgeni River.

Botanic Gardens

Among the most attractive of the city's green areas are the Botanic Gardens, whose camelias and azaleas put on a memorable springtime show. Here you'll also find a variety of splendid trees (including Moreton Bay fig, cypress and camphor), an avenue lined with stately planes, a lake, a 24-ha (59-acre) indigenous section that sustains a wealth of KwaZulu-Natal mist-belt plants, and a restaurant. The gardens, located off

The endangered Hilton daisy.

Mayor's Walk, about 4 km (2½ miles) from the city centre, are open daily 08h00 to 18h00 (17h00 in winter).

WILDLIFE ON VIEW

There are a number of fine game parks and nature reserves within a 30-km (20-mile) radius of Pietermaritzburg. Notable among these are:

Queen Elizabeth Park

About 8 km (5 miles) to the north-west of the city (via Duncan MacKenzie Drive) is Queen Elizabeth Park, headquarters of the Natal Parks Board and sanctuary for game animals (white rhino among them), indigenous and exotic plants (of special interest are the cycads and endangered Hilton daisies) and a variety of birds. There are picnic and barbecue sites, viewing hides, trails and a curio shop. Entrance is free of charge; open daily 06h00 to 18h00. For central reservations; tel. (0331) 47-1981.

Game Valley

Located in the scenic Karkloof Valley, some 20 km (12½ miles) from the city along the Greytown road (R33), is Game Valley – a haven for a myriad birds, for breeding herds of white rhino and for Cape buffalo, giraffe, rare roan and sable antelope and many more. This is also a magically scenic forest and grassland conservancy, its centrepiece KwaZulu-Natal's highest waterfall: the Karkloof Falls. Accommodation is available in a luxurious country lodge, and day visitors are also welcome. For more information; tel. (033) 569-1787.

BATTLEFIELDS ROUTE

During much of the 19th century the Midlands and northern KwaZulu-Natal were an immense battleground, savagely contested during a hundred years of strife, stained with the blood of countless warriors. It was here that Shaka's newly created armies fashioned the Zulu kingdom, later waging war against the Voortrekkers (1838) and the British (1879), here that Britain challenged the independence of the Transvaal (1880–81) and here that some of the most bitter fighting of the Anglo-Boer War (1899–1902) took place. Visitors with an interest in matters military will find endless fascination along the Battlefields Route, an itinerary that takes you to the major sites. For details, contact Durban Unlimited (see p 62).

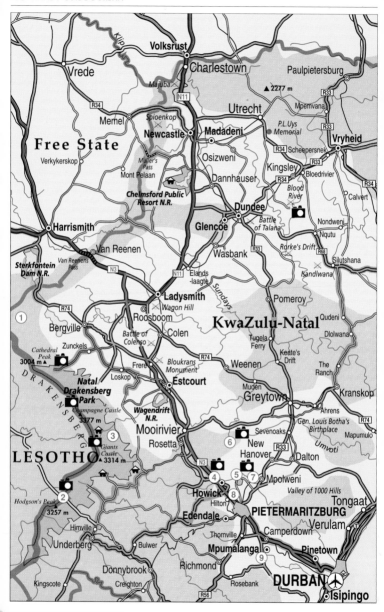

Trailists enjoying the 5-day 'Giant's Cup' trail.

Visitors have a number of accommodation options, including the Karos Mont-aux-Sources, Little Switzerland and Royal Natal National Park hotels, two park camps (bungalows, cottages and a luxury lodge) and a caravan-camping ground in the next-door Rugged Glen reserve. Contact the Natal Parks Board or the Drakensberg Publicity Association (*see* p 62) for further details on accommodation. The reserve's major access point from the south is Bergville, on the R74.

CENTRAL 'BERG

In the central section, within the extensive Drakensberg Park, are **Cathedral Peak**, a complex that embraces some of the range's most challenging heights, **Champagne Castle**, whose summit at 3 377 m (11 200 ft), is the country's highest point, **Cathkin Peak**, a massive 3 181 m (10 590 ft) detached formation that looks over dense forest plantations, **Ndedema Gorge,** known for its San rock paintings, and further to the south, the enormous basalt bulk of **Giant's Castle**. Winterton, on the R74, serves as a convenient gateway to the Cathedral Peak–Champagne Castle area, while Giant's Castle can be reached via a number of roads branching off the N3.

SAN LEGACY
Both **Ndedema** and *Giant's Castle* are renowned for the caves and rock shelters that were once haven to the long-gone San or Bushmen of the region and which are extensively and beautifully decorated with the work of these remarkable artists. The Ndedema area embraces more than 17 'galleries' that, between them, hold approximately 4 000 paintings. More accessible to the ordinary visitor, though, is the cave art display in a site museum in the Giant's Castle Game Reserve (see p 52).

Giant's Castle camp: an idyllic holiday location.

▼ Giant's Castle Game Reserve

The 3 325-m-high (11 080 ft) Giant's Castle is the centrepiece of this reserve that was originally created to protect the eland but is now noted more for its breathtaking scenery, its flowering plants, its wide variety of animal life and its rock art. Of particular interest to visitors, and a stone's throw away from the rest camp, is the Main Cave site museum. The museum contains more than 540 San rock paintings together with life-sized models of these remarkable artists. Bird enthusiasts can observe the rare lammergeyer and other birds of prey from a hide in the game reserve. Accommodation is offered in cottages and in a caravan park; bookings to be made through the Natal Parks Board; tel. (0331) 47-1981.

Rock art depicting the thrill of the hunt.

SOUTHERN 'BERG

Principal features of the southern 'Berg are the famed Sani Pass, the pretty little villages of Bulwer, Himeville and Underberg and a quartet of scenic nature reserves noted for their troutwaters. To get there, turn off the N3 at Howick and follow the R617 Bulwer road. Alternatively, book your place on the Drakensberg Express, a daily mini-bus service that links Durban and Pietermaritzburg with all the southern Drakensberg resorts; tel. (031) 32-4945.

Sani Pass

The only high road linking KwaZulu-Natal with the mountain kingdom of Lesotho, to the west, climbs over the Sani ('Bushman') Pass at the southern end of the Drakensberg. The route is really too steep for anything other than four-wheel-drive vehicles and the sturdy little ponies of the conical-hatted Sotho, but it's worth making the ascent for the wondrous peak-and-valley vistas that unfold. Mokhotlong Mountain Transport offers daily tours up Sani Pass; tel. (033) 702-1206.

AGFA

PHOTO TIP

When filming in the more rural country areas of KwaZulu-Natal, especially when it comes to 'ethnic' subjects (villagers in traditional dress, for example), it's good manners to seek permission beforehand from the village headman or from whoever else is in charge locally. Etiquette also demands that you offer the subject a small cash gratuity.

The Sani Pass: it's steep, so go by four-wheel-drive or on a pony trek to enjoy the superb vistas.

AGFA

PHOTO TIP

Traditional Zulu villages, such as Shakaland and Dumazulu, have been specially created for the benefit of the tourist. These villages provide opportunities for those keen on capturing traditional Zulu life on film. At Shakaland, for example, one can film anything from pottery-making and dancing to spear-throwing and beer-brewing. It is, however, good manners first to ask your subject's permission should you wish to get some good close-up photos.

DUMAZULU KRAAL

DumaZulu Kraal, 15 km (9½ miles) south of Hluhluwe village (turn off the N2 at the Bushlands off-ramp), offers a 'cultural experience' that takes in the world of the sangoma, Zulu dancing and domestic crafts such as the making of spears, shields, baskets and pots. Other attractions include a curio shop and a Zulu eating house and shebeen where visitors can sample traditional Zulu food and drink. Tour packages that are offered also include visits to the region's major game areas; tel. (035) 562-0343.

ZULU HERITAGE

Make your way north of the Tugela River, into the historic region of Zululand, and you'll find a myriad reminders of an earlier, more colourful and perhaps prouder age. The old ways of the Zulu are disappearing, and what remains of the past tends to be at its most visible, and accessible, in a number of 'living museums' specially created for the tourist. These include Fort Nongqai (just to the west of Eshowe), which houses the Zululand Historical Museum; the cultural centre – and its reconstruction of the enormous Zulu royal 'residence' – at Ondini, near Ulundi; DumaZulu Kraal, near Hluhluwe village, and, perhaps the most impressive of all, Shakaland.

Shakaland

At Shakaland, which featured in the television epics *Shaka Zulu* and *John Ross*, overnight visitors stay in one of the hotel's 100-plus beehive huts (they have all the modern conveniences), sample Zulu food and drink, watch traditional dancing, listen to the praise singer, observe a sangoma, a herbalist and a hut-builder at work, and view a wide range of craft displays. From Eshowe, follow the R68 northwards for 14 km (9 miles), turn left onto the Goedgetrou gravel road; Shakaland is 3.5 km (2 miles) further on. Day and overnight package tours are available; tel. (03546) 912.

An inyanga at work with his umuthi.

NORTHERN KWAZULU-NATAL GAME SANCTUARIES

The KwaZulu-Natal wildlife areas – those in the historic region of Zululand to the north of the Tugela River (take the N2 through Mtubatuba) – are among the world's finest. A warm climate, good rains (in most years), a remarkable diversity of grasses, shrubs and trees and an admirable dedication to conservation combine to sustain ideal habitats for great numbers of animals and birds.

HLUHLUWE-UMFOLOZI PARK

The park combines two of Africa's oldest conservation areas: they were born in 1897, about a year before the Kruger National Park made its appearance. They are also as richly endowed as the better-known northern sanctuary: far smaller in size, they nevertheless contain almost 70 per cent of the Kruger's animal and plant species. The park's two sec-

The white rhino – saved from extinction.

tions are somewhat different in character, though they do of course have much in common. Bookings can be made through the Natal Parks Board; tel. (0331) 47-1981.

♥ Hluhluwe

Hluhluwe, the smaller of the two sections, is a stunningly beautiful expanse of grass-covered hills, misty woodlands and dense riverine forest that combine to sustain more than 80 different kinds of mammal, including the 'big five' and an impressive 425 bird species. For visitors, there are about 100 km (62 miles) of game-viewing roads, an inviting auto-trail, a walking trail and comfortable self-catering accommodation at the extensive Hilltop rest camp. Hluhluwe also boasts an exclusive lodge and the charming little Muntulu bush-camp.

♥ Umfolozi

The Umfolozi section covers more than 50 000 ha (123 550 acres) of sweetly-grassed, well-watered savanna and lush floodplain. Its wildlife is much the same as that of Hluhluwe; recommended is its auto-trail; accommodation is in hutted rest camps and bush camps.

♥ ***RHINO RESCUE***
The Hluhluwe-Umfolozi Park is renowned for its rhinos. It was here that the two species of this massive primeval animal (the white, a gentle grazer, and its smaller and rather more agressive black cousin, which is a browser) were nurtured away from the brink of extinction in a decades-long campaign launched by the Natal Parks Board. So successful was the effort that surplus animals began to be translocated to other reserves in and beyond South Africa. The park is currently home to 2 000 white and 400 black rhino.

GREATER ST LUCIA WETLAND PARK

The huge St Lucia complex, on the warm and humid Indian Ocean seaboard north of Durban and rated among the world's leading wetland and marine conservancies, is a remarkable ecological compound of lake, lagoon, marshland, forest, high coastal dune, pristine shoreline, limpid ocean and offshore coral reef.

The proclaimed area stretches 140 km (90 miles) from the Umfolozi River mouth northwards to Sodwana Bay; from Durban one gets there along the N2, branching off at either Mtubatuba or Hluhluwe village.

Accommodation is plentiful, ranging from fairly basic huts through well-equipped self-catering chalets to comfortable lodges. Bookings can be made through the Natal Parks Board; tel. (0331) 47-1981.

Lake St Lucia

The park's focus is a shallow 'lake' – in reality an extended estuarine system fringed by reeds and, especially in the north, by marshes – that supports an astounding diversity of aquatic life forms (including crocodile and hippo) and birds, among them white pelicans, flamingos, Caspian terns, saddlebills, spoonbills, the ubiquitous African fish eagle, herons (12 different species) and many others.

The peaceful waterland of St Lucia at dawn.

The northern part of the lake extends into a separate stretch of water known as False Bay, along whose western perimeter is the vast **False Bay Park**. Here you'll be able to spot some of the 280 species of wetland, forest and bushveld bird that have been identified, together with mammals such as duiker, reedbuck, the shy suni antelope, the handsome shaggy-coated nyala, the spotted hyaena and the warthog.

Amenities at False Bay, **Charter's Creek** and **Fanies Island** comprise fully equipped rest huts, camp sites, fishing spots, boat hire and superb self-guided walks.

Mkuzi's pans offer good game viewing.

Mkuzi Game Reserve

This vast expanse of grassland, evergreen forest and marsh to the north of Lake St Lucia is famed for its floral wealth (ghostly fever trees and giant sycamore figs are prominent) and for its 300 or so bird species.

Many of the latter can be seen on and around the Nsumu and other pans, or shallow lakelets, where viewing hides have been established. Resident animals include black rhino, giraffe, leopard, cheetah, crocodile, hippo, eland and other antelope. Self-catering accommodation is provided in the pleasant Mantuma camp, Mkumbi hunting lodge and in the Nhlonhlela bush lodge. Nhlonhlela's open-sided dining enclosure and observation platform, overlooking the pan, is especially attractive. Access from Durban is via Hluhluwe village.

PIONEER RESERVE
*Pride of northern Zululand's private conservancies and an excellent eco-tourism destination is the **Phinda Resource Reserve** near the St Lucia Wetland Park. Here there's luxurious lodge accommodation, a profusion of wildlife habitats and a stunning diversity of animals (the 'big five' apart from the buffalo) and birds. Phinda is a pioneer in the conservation field, living proof that the priceless natural heritage can be used to the benefit of all – the wildlife, the farmers, the local communities and the tourists. Book through the central reservations office; tel. (011) 803-8421.*

FOSSIL FINDS
*The western shores and the **False Bay** area of St Lucia have been found to be immensely rich in fossils. Large creatures called ammonites, related to the modern octopus, swam in the sea here 90 millon years ago, aeons before the ocean levels changed and the region became a coastal plain, and the area is now a treasure-trove of their shells. Relics include shark's teeth the size of a man's hand and an ancient coral reef.*

Cape Vidal encompasses the tranquil Lake Bhangazi.

LAND OF LAKES

The far northern coastal parts of KwaZulu-Natal, a region known as Maputaland, is distinguished by it lovely lakes. **Sibaya** extends across 70 km² (45 miles²) and is South Africa's largest stretch of fresh water, nurturing hippos and crocodiles and a myriad birds. Further north is a chain of lakes and mangrove swamps separated from the sea by gigantic dunes. This is **Kosi Bay**, a vast tropical paradise of intensely blue water, marshlands and forests of sycamore fig, raffia, wild date and lala palm. The reserve is popular for its lakeside and estuary fishing spots, its superb bird life (notably herons, palmnut vultures and the African fish eagles), its walking trails and its luxury lodges.

St Lucia Village

Located at the 'lake's' estuary, this little one-street village is the commercial hub of the area, boasting a variety of services, shops and places to stay (including a hotel and three camp sites). Recreational opportunities abound: rock and surf angling, skiboating, lake fishing, sightseeing cruises on the *Santa Lucia* (*see* p 56), game-viewing at a small game reserve just north of the village, and a number of trails.

Here, too, is the **Crocodile Centre,** which houses an impressive collection of these giant reptiles, most of them common Nile crocodiles, though the place is also home to the dwarf and long-snouted varieties, both of which are threatened species indigenous to equatorial Africa. The centre is open daily 07h00 to 17h30. Access to St Lucia village is from Mtubatuba.

Cape Vidal

This attractive little resort lies on the coast 30 km (20 miles) north of St Lucia village. The surrounding countryside and that of the Mfabeni section is covered by marshy grasslands and forest, a pristine area that sustains great numbers of water-loving reedbuck together with buffalo, kudu, duiker, jackal, the occasional shy leopard and a wealth of dune-forest bird species.

Cape Vidal is especially popular as a ski-boat venue, and accommodation is in log cabins, a bush camp and camp site. Access is via Mtubatuba and St Lucia Village.

Sodwana's blue sea hides offshore coral reefs.

AGFA
PHOTO TIP

South Africa's game parks are a photographer's paradise – and not just because of their free-roaming large mammals. You'll find the smaller creatures (birds, vervet monkeys, rodents, lizards and so forth) are often unusually tame around the rest camps. They provide excellent subject matter for close-up work – quite literally on your doorstep.

Sodwana Bay

This small park and its resort hug the St Lucia marine reserve in the far north – and play host to a multitude of summertime holidaymakers. The bay, its lovely beaches, the warm ocean and the offshore coral reefs are a magnet for scuba-divers and ski-boat anglers; superb catches of barracuda, tuna, blue and black marlin and other game species are routinely recorded.

Most visitors stay at the caravan-camping complex, though accommodation is also available in log cabins and in a luxury lodge outside the park. Facilities include a small grocery store, fish-weighing points, fish-freezers and boat storage. Despite the human presence, the area remains a tranquil and unspoilt home to several antelope such as reedbuck, steenbok, duiker and an array of birds, while the beaches are nesting grounds for turtles. Access is via Mkuze (or the Lower Mkuze Road) to Mbazwana, and then south, following the signs.

TURTLES ON VIEW

The giant, gentle, cumbersome loggerhead and leatherback turtles that visit the northern beaches migrate immense distances to lay their eggs – remarkably, in the very patch of sand on which they themselves were born! The female locates the precise spot by scent, then drops her clutch, disguises the nest and makes her weary way back to the sea. The hatchlings emerge after 70 days to face the hungry predators of beach and ocean; very few survive to return as adults. At Sodwana Bay, guided night-drives are offered during the months of December and January; bookings through the Natal Parks Board; tel. (053) 571-0051/2/3.

The rare leatherback turtle.

VISITOR'S DIGEST

GETTING THERE

By Air
Durban International Airport is about 15 km to the south of the city centre and handles regional and domestic as well as international flights. Banking, currency and car rental facilities are also available. A shuttle bus provides a 24-hour service between the airport, the city and beachfront hotels. The city terminal is on the corner of Smith and Aliwal streets. For information regarding arrival and departure times; tel. 42-6111.

By Road
National highways, generally in excellent condition, link Durban with all major South African centres. The N2 leads south and then east through Port Elizabeth to Cape Town, and north past KwaZulu-Natal's many game sanctuaries to Swaziland; the N3 takes you northwest through Pietermaritzburg and Harrismith to Johannesburg.

By Rail
Intercity railway passenger services connect Durban with Johannesburg and Cape Town. The main railway station is in Umgeni Road, to the north of the city centre. Arrival and departure enquiries; tel. 361-7621.

GETTING AROUND

Car Hire
The major international rental companies are well represented in Durban, and car-hire facilities are also offered by several local firms. Consult the Yellow Pages or enquire at hotel reception.

City Travel
An adequate municipal bus service covers the metropolitan area. **Mynah** mini-buses transports visitors between the central area and the beachfront; the **Tuk-Tuk** three-wheelers take you through the city and to specific points along the Golden Mile. Durban's **taxis** do not cruise the streets in search of fares but confine themselves to permanent ranks; taxi companies are listed in the Yellow Pages.

Coach Services
Coaches operating between South Africa's major centres are: **Greyhound Citiliner:** tel. 361-7774; **Skyliner Tours:** tel. 301-1550; **Spoornet:** tel. 361-2030 and **Translux Express:** tel. 361-8333.

GENERAL INFORMATION

Climate
Durban's weather is nearly always kind to holidaymakers, although summer humidity levels can be uncomfortably high. The average daily maximum temperature during summertime (January) hovers around the 27 °C (80 °F) mark, falling to 20 °C (68 °F) in the cooler hours. The average winter (July) maximum temperature is approximately 22 °C (72 °F), the minimum a tolerable 11 °C (50 °F). The city receives more than 1 000 mm (40 in) of rainfall a year, most of it in summertime during regular torrential tropical downpours. For more information on the weather: tel. 307-4121.

Electricity
South Africa's electricity supply is rated at 220/230 volts AC at 50 cycles per second. Plugs are 5-amp, two-pin or 15-amp three-pin (round plugs).

Health Hazards
Sunstroke and **sunburn** are extremely dangerous and visitors are strongly advised to apply block-out creams and to avoid lengthy exposure to the sun, especially during the hottest period of the day which is from 12h00 until 15h00.
Malaria is endemic in northern Zululand. It is therefore essential that you consult a medical practitioner or pharmacist to obtain the necessary preventative medication prior to visiting these infested areas.

Measurement
South Africa uses the metric system.

Medical Services

Visitors are responsible for their own arrangements, and are advised to take out medical insurance prior to departure. Private doctors are listed in the telephone directory under 'Medical Practitioners'. Hospitalization is usually arranged through a private doctor, but in an emergency you may telephone or go directly to the casualty department of a general hospital.

Money

South Africa's currency is the rand (R), which is divided into 100 cents (c). Coins are issued in denominations of 1c, 2c, 5c, 10c, 20c, 50c, R1, R2 and R5; notes are in denominations of R10, R20, R50, R100 and R200.

Currency exchange: At commercial banks and at various bueaux de change. Traveller's cheques and international credit cards are widely accepted. Note that petrol cannot be purchased by credit card.

Tipping: Provided you're satisfied with the service, it's usual to tip waiters and taxi drivers 10 to 15 per cent. For non-quantifiable services (porters, room attendants and so forth), it is customary to offer between R2 and R5. Tipping petrol attendants is optional, but a window wash and a friendly smile do deserve recognition.

Service charges: Hotels are forbidden to levy a general charge but there are often heavy telephone surcharges so check your hotel bill carefully. Restaurants may levy a service charge but few choose to do so.

Security

The crime rate in and around Durban is relatively high, the product (largely) of widespread unemployment and of political and social instability created by rapid political transition. Visitors are advised to take the following precautions:

* Do not walk alone at night in either the city or in the suburbs. The beachfront is safe if you're with a group, but avoid deserted and poorer areas.
* Do not carry large amounts of money around with you and avoid wearing expensive jewellery.

* Try not to look or conduct yourself like a tourist. Cameras and bulging pocket-books are magnets for muggers.
* Do not keep valuables in your hotel room; use a safety deposit box.
* Beware of carjackers. Keep your car doors locked when driving, and ensure your windows are up, especially at intersections. Drive on if given cause for suspicion; do not argue if confronted.

Trading Hours

Banks are open weekdays 09h00 to 15h30, Saturdays 09h00 to 11h00. Most also operate a nationwide network of Automatic Teller Machines (ATMs) offering a 24-hour service.

Post Offices are open weekdays 08h00 to 16h30, Saturdays 08h00 to 13h00. Postage stamps are available at corner cafés, stationery shops and supermarkets.

Retail outlets are open weekdays 08h30 (09h00 in some cases) to 17h00, Saturdays 08h30 to 13h00. Supermarkets tend to close later (18h00) and most are open on Saturday afternoons, Sunday mornings and on the mornings of some public holidays. Some of the larger beachfront and central shopping complexes are open till late, as are many small neighbourhood cafés. Liquor outlets usually close at 18h30.

Shopping

A 14 per cent value-added tax (VAT) is built into the price of all goods except a few food items. The international exchange rate is highly favourable, and prices are generally comparable (and in many instances much lower) to those in many other industrially advanced countries. Local products of particular interest include gold, diamond and semi-precious stone jewellery; leatherwork (including crocodile and ostrich skin items); African handcrafts (notably printed fabrics, tapestries, rugs, wood carvings, basketry and beadwork).

Telecommunications

The country's telephone system is fully automatic, and one can dial direct to most parts of the world. Telephone directories list all local and international dialling codes as well as rates (the international dialling code for South Africa is #27; the code for Durban is 031). Should you find that a number you need is not listed, or that the number has changed, dial Enquiries at 1023. Public phones are coin- or card-operated; phone cards can be purchased at most cafés, stationery shops and supermarkets. Cellular telephones are a prominent feature of the local communications scene, as is E-mail. Facsimile transmission (fax) services are also widely available.

Time

South African Standard Time is two hours ahead of Greenwich Mean (or Universal Standard) Time; one hour ahead of Central European Winter Time; seven hours ahead of the USA's Eastern Standard Winter Time.

Tourist Information

The city's principal information authority is **Durban Unlimited**, whose main offices are on the ground floor of Tourist Junction, 160 Pine Street; tel. 304-4934, fax. 304-3868. Open Monday to Saturday during business hours. Durban Unlimited also maintains a presence on the beachfront (next to Sea World, Marine Parade; tel. 32-2608) and at Durban's International Airport; tel. 42-0400. **Satour** (South African Tourism Board), whose offices are located in the Marine Building, 22 Gardiner Street, provide information on the local and national touring scene; tel. 304-7144, fax. 305-6693.
Regional publicity associations include:
* **Amanzimtoti;** tel. 903-7498
* **Drakensberg;** tel. (036) 448-1557 (northern & central) or (033) 701-1096 (southern)
* **Howick;** tel. (0332) 30-5305
* **North Coast;** tel. (0322) 6-1997
* **Pietermaritzburg;** tel. (0331) 45-1348
* **South Coast;** tel. (0323) 2-1364 (Scottburgh); tel. (03931) 2-2322 (Margate)
* **Thukela Joint Services Board** (Drakensberg/Midlands areas); tel. (0361) 31-0236
* **Zululand Joint Services Board** (northern KwaZulu-Natal region); tel. (0351) 4-1404
* **Umhlanga Rocks;** tel. 561-4257

WHERE TO STAY

5- and 4-star hotels
Crowne Plaza, North Beach; tel. 37-1321, fax. 32-5527.
Holiday Inn, Marine Parade; tel. 37-3341, fax. 32-9885.
Karos Edward Hotel, Marine Parade; tel. 37-3681, fax. 32-1692.
The Royal Hotel, central; tel. 304-0331, fax. 307-6884.
Tropicana, Marine Parade; tel. 368-1511, fax. 368-2322.

3-star hotels
Beach Hotel, Marine Parade; tel. 37-4222, fax. 368-2322.
Blue Waters Hotel, Marine Parade; tel. 32-4272, fax. 37-5817.
Holiday Inn Garden Court, North Beach; tel. 32-7361, fax. 37-4058.
Holiday Inn Garden Court, South Beach; tel. 37-2231, fax. 37-4640.
Palace Protea Hotel, Marine Parade; tel. 32-8351, fax. 32-8307.

Self-catering and Budget
A number of holiday and executive apartments, resort cottages, country lodges, guest houses and bed-and-breakfast establishments, as well as youth hostels, are available in Greater Durban. Contact Durban Unlimited (*see* left) or your travel agent for the wider options.

WHERE TO EAT

Amigos, Westville Pavilion; Mexican food; tel. 265-0646.
Api Taki, central; Indonesian, Chinese and Malaysian menu; tel. 307-1847.
Cachèt, central; wonderful international cuisine; plus atmospheric bistro café on balcony; tel. 301-3807/8.
Christina's, Musgrave; international, French Provençal undertones; tel. 303-2111.
Egoli, central; traditional German cuisine; tel. 32-5863.
Kanders House of Curry, beachfront; tel. 368-2250.

La Dolce Vita, central; international menu; tel. 301-3347.

Le Trouquet, Cowies Hill; French provençal cuisine; tel. 86-5388.

Lord Nelson, central; seafood; steaks are a speciality; also pub lunches; tel. 37-8332.

Lord Prawn, beachfront; steak and seafood specialities; tel. 37-2978.

Maharaj, beachfront; variety of curry dishes; tel. 37-3451.

O'Cacador, beachfront; Portuguese menu; tel. 37-7214.

Oliver Twist, central; international menu; tel. 37-4055.

The Orient, beachfront; Cantonese and Malaysian dishes; tel. 37-2083.

Pink Panther, beachfront; international menu; tel. 37-3381.

Roma Revolving Restaurant, *see* p 24.

Royal Grill, Royal Hotel (central); faultless cuisine and service; tel. 304-0331.

Taj Mahal, central; Indian dishes; strictly halaal; tel. 305-3859.

Tartan Dog, beachfront; lively pub; à la carte menu; tel. 32-0216.

Thatcher's, beachfront; atmospheric pub; à la carte menu; live music; tel. 37-4311.

Ulundi, Royal Hotel (central); Indian cuisine; tel. 304-0331.

Victoria Bar & Restaurant, Point Road; wonderful pub meals; seafood and chicken are specialities; tel. 37-4645.

TOURS & EXCURSIONS

Hamba Kahle, guided township tours; tel. 305-5586.

Itchy Feet, custom-made tours to game reserves and the Drakensberg; various adventure tours also available, these include white-water rafting, abseiling, paragliding, water-skiing, scuba-diving, hiking, mountain-biking; tel. 561-1125.

Rave Vacation Tours, personalized tours, covering both Durban and KwaZulu-Natal; tel. (083) 253-4545.

Shaka Tours & Safaris, excursions to game reserves, Shakaland, Valley of a Thousand Hills, Sani Pass and aboard the Banana Express steam train; tel. 561-2860.

Strelitzia Tours, cover the Valley of a Thousand Hills, KwaZulu-Natal Midlands, Zululand game sanctuaries, Battlefields, South Coast (also the Banana Express), Drakensberg and the Kruger National Park; special-interest tours available (diving, deep-sea fishing, golf); tel. 86-1904.

Sun Ride, offer luxury tours to various game sanctuaries, the Valley of a Thousand Hills, the Wild Coast Sun Casino, the Drakensberg, Shakaland traditional village and the Kruger National Park; tel. 561-2522.

Tour-A-Vista, tours on offer include the Valley of a Thousand Hills, Howick Falls and Pietermaritzburg; tel. 72-2031.

Tugela Safaris, covers various Zululand game reserves, Lake St Lucia, bird-watching tours, Sani Pass, Swaziland and the Kruger National Park; tel. 303-2548.

U-Tours, a wide variety of tours on offer, including daily trips to the Wild Coast Sun Casino; tel. 368-2848.

Valley Express, budget tours to the Valley of a Thousand Hills; tel. 86-6831.

Zulwini Tours & Safaris, covers various Zululand game sanctuaries and KwaZulu-Natal Midlands; tel. 307-1567.

USEFUL CONTACT NUMBERS

Addington Hospital: tel. 32-2111.

Ambulance: tel. 1-0177 (national number).

Automobile Association: tel. 301-0341.

Chemists, emergency: tel. 368-3666 (Durban beachfront); tel. 47-4990 (The Bluff); tel. 83-8483 (Durban North).

Citizens' Advice Bureau: tel. 304-5548.

Computicket: tel. 304-2753.

Fire Brigade: tel. 309-3333.

Life Line: (equivalent to British Samaritans) tel. 23-2323.

Medical emergencies: tel. 301-3737.

Natal Parks Board: tel. (0331) 47-1981. (bookings); tel. (0331) 47-1891 (enquiries).

Police Flying Squad: tel. 1-0111 (this is a national number).

Police charge office: tel. 32-2322.

Sea Rescue: tel. 37-2200.

Tourist Information: *see* page 62.

Visa enquiries: tel. 301-5803.

INDEX